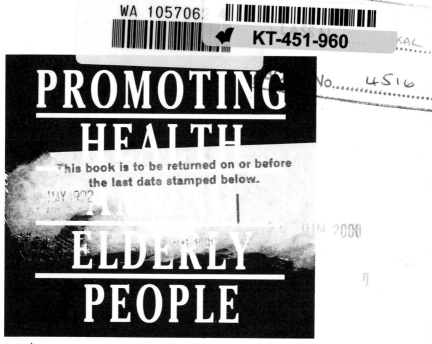

PROMOTING

HEALTH

ELDERLY

PEOPLE

A Statement from a Working Group

Programme on Epidemiology of
Ageing
London School of Hygiene
and Tropical Medicine

Age Concern Institute of
Gerontology
King's College London

King's Fund Institute

© King Edward's Hospital Fund for London 1988

Published on behalf of the London School of Hygiene and Tropical Medicine, Age Concern Institute of Gerontology, King's College London and the King's Fund Institute

Designed, typeset, printed and bound by Redesign, London

ISBN 1 870551 86 9

British Library Cataloguing in Publication Data

Kalache, Alex
Promoting Health Among Elderly People.
I. Britain. Health Promotion. Old Persons.
II. Title II. Warnes, Tony.
III. Hunter, David J.

King's Fund Publishing Office
14 Palace Court
London W2 4HT

CONTENTS

PREFACE

Ageing is associated with health unless there is sickness or disability. Some ill health and disabilities can be prevented. When this is not possible, the majority of problems are dealt with through self care, with support from relatives and friends. When these support systems fail, proper diagnosis and treatment may be required.

The main focus of health promotion in old age rests, therefore, with individuals within their environments, with health professionals playing a vital role in transferring knowledge and adapting skills so as to enhance the possibility of meaningful, autonomous and satisfying lives for elderly people within their communities. It is perfectly possible to be both old and healthy and the majority of elderly people are living proof of this.

This report is aimed at all those concerned with the wellbeing of elderly people in the United Kingdom, present and future. In other words, this report concerns all of us and it is hoped that it will serve as a catalyst for new ideas in the promotion of healthy ageing.

Dr Alex Kalache,
Programme on Epidemiology of Ageing,
London School of Hygiene and Tropical Medicine

Dr Tony Warnes,
Senior Research Associate,
Age Concern Institute of Gerontology,
King's College London

Dr David J Hunter,
Health Policy Analyst,
King's Fund Institute,
London

1988

ACKNOWLEDGEMENTS

The coordinators of the *Promoting Health Among Elderly People* project wish to thank the following organisations for their invaluable support in the production of this report: the Helen Hamlyn Foundation, King Edward's Hospital Fund for London, the World Health Organization, Age Concern England, and Help the Aged.

FOREWORD

In May 1986 the World Health Organization (WHO) Programme for Health of the Elderly convened in Hamilton, Canada an Advisory Group Meeting on Health Promotion in Old Age. The scope of the meeting was restricted to opportunities within the primary health care sector for screening and early detection of diseases in old age. One of its main recommendations was a direct call to member states to prepare national plans of action on the subject

The origins of this report and of the working group established to help in its preparation lie in the WHO initiative. But there was already growing interest in activities which might, in one way or another, help more elderly people to live full lives in their communities. The WHO call provided the catalyst. The enthusiastic response of those invited to join the working group at different stages is testimony to this.

Work on the report was jointly coordinated by the Department of Community Health, London School of Hygiene and Tropical Medicine; the Age Concern Institute of Gerontology at King's College London; and the King's Fund Institute. It proceeded in three stages:

1. The preparation of a consultation document by a small study group composed of individuals drawn from organisations concerned with the welfare aand health of elderly people throughout the United Kingdom (for a list of participants and programme see Appendix 1). The study group met in Harrogate from 4-6 February 1987. On the basis of its deliberations a preliminary document was prepared and subsequently redrafted for circulation within the group.

2. A modified group met again at a second workshop held at the King's Fund Institute in London on 7 April 1987 (for a list of participants see Appendix 1). The aim was to discuss the document and produce a revised version which would be circulated more widely, inviting comments and participation in a national one day workshop.

3. The national workshop was held at the King's Fund Centre, London on 5 October 1987. It was attended by individuals representing a wide range of organisations (for a list of participants and programme see Appendix 2). The main task was to examine the document which had arisen from the previous workshops, and subsequently to

incorporate the reactions and suggestions of both those present and other individuals who were unable to attend the meeting.

The whole exercise proved instructive and illuminating for all concerned. Given the great variety of backgrounds and perspectives brought to bear on the issues under discussion by the members of the workshop, it was unlikely that we would achieve a consensus. Nor did we. However, we believe that the fruits of the many discussions conducted over the year which are presented in this document have profited from a lively exchange of diverse views. They reflect the present state of debate about health promotion and ageing in the United Kingdom.

We are indebted to all those who took part for their time, their ideas and, most important, their enthusiastic participation in this venture.

The document is offered not as a final statement but rather as a contribution to a continuing debate on how best to promote the health of elderly people in all its many complex dimensions. Final responsibility for what appears rests with the authors. Not every participant subscribes to every statement in this account. In bringing together in a single document a range of policy and service concerns, supported wherever possible by factual material and examples, we have attempted to provide a useful practical resource upon which service providers, managers and planners, at whom it is primarily aimed, will draw.

It is often said that little innovation takes place in services for older people. If nothing else, this document should dispel that belief. The field of health promotion and older people is alive with new initiatives. It is vital for policy and organisational learning that these are documented and evaluated independently so that the best can be diffused more widely. By publishing this report, we claim no more than having taken a first and modest step towards this goal.

Plan of Report

Following an introductory section setting out the WHO approach to health promotion, the report is organised in three parts. Part One presents a brief review of health trends across selected countries and identifies the challenge for health promotion and ageing in the United Kingdom. Part Two sets out the action required by different agencies and groups at all levels of government and beyond in order to meet the challenge. Part Three provides examples of innovative projects collected during the deliberations on the report. The examples illustrate the range and diversity of new initiatives across the country. They show what is possible, although for proven schemes to be disseminated more widely we propose that evaluation needs more commonly to be an integral element of a project.

INTRODUCTION

In 1981 a Planning Committee was established at the World Health Organization (WHO) Regional Office for Europe to look at new approaches for the maintenance of health. By January 1984 a programme on 'Health Promotion' had been created. Since then, a number of activities involving professionals as well as consumers have taken place which have clarified the distinctive approach of this programme. The approach is briefly outlined in this introductory section.

The WHO Approach to Health Promotion

The development of priorities and practices for health promotion for a nation depends upon the prevailing economic and cultural conditions; these differ from country to country and from region to region. Yet fundamental tenets apply anywhere. Basic resources for the health of any individual are income, shelter and food. Without a solid foundation of these basic necessities, the improvement of health is an abstraction. Complementary requisites are:

● information/knowledge about health factors

● appropriate skills to promote health

● supportive environments to enhance health

● opportunities for healthier choices.

All of these can be encapsulated within the concept of a total environment (with its economic, physical, social and cultural dimensions) which may enhance health.

WHO's concept of health promotion emerged from the need for change in both the ways *and* conditions of living. On the one hand this requires the participation of all people in the development of their health, and on the other, a commitment to the total environment conducive to health: personal choice combined with social responsibility to create a healthier future.

Principles

The underlying idea is that people should be able to increase their control over their health. This should lead automatically to an improvement in health. Health is seen as a positive resource for everyday life emphasising simultaneously physical capacities as well as social and personal resources. In order to enjoy 'good health' individuals have to realise at least some of their aspirations, be able to satisfy their needs and cope with their living environments. There are five principles.

- Health promotion involves the population as a whole in the context of the everyday life of people, rather than focusing on people at risk for specific diseases. This requires full and continuing access to information about health by all the population, using whatever dissemination methods are available.

- Health promotion is directed towards action on the determinants or causes of health. An intersectoral approach is required with governments (at both local and national levels) having a unique responsibility to act appropriately.

- Health promotion involves the population as a whole in the context of the everyday life of people, rather than focusing on people at risk for specific diseases. This requires full and continuing access to information about health by all the population, using whatever dissemination methods are available.

- Health promotion aims particularly at effective and concrete public participation, both individually and collectively.

- While health promotion is not a medical service, health professionals — particularly in primary health care — have an important role in nurturing and enabling it.

Subject Areas

Given these basic principles an almost unlimited list of issues for health promotion could be generated including: food policy, housing, coping mechanisms, social networks and so on. Suggested general subject areas are:

Access to health

Inequalities need to be reduced and public policies reoriented to the maintenance and development of health in the population regardless of current health status.

Development of an environment conducive to health

Such an environment is dynamic and ever-changing; continuous monitoring and the assessment of trends and changes in factors affecting health are essential.

Strengthening of social networks and social support
Behaviour and attitudes relevant to health are largely determined by social relationships which are also crucial for successful individual coping strategies.

Society's predominant way of life
Personal behaviour as well as beliefs and values are all fostered by predominant lifestyles which can be shaped in a way more conducive to health, provided that respect for personal coping mechanisms is observed.

Increasing knowledge about health
Informed choices have to be based on knowledge derived from sources such as: epidemiological and sociological studies on patterns of health and factors affecting them; the public's perceptions and experiences of health; experiences in other locations that might be of 'local' relevance and so on. In the dissemination of this accumulated knowledge the mass media and new information technologies play a vital role.

Priorities for the Development of Policies

While governments, through public policy, have a special responsibility to ensure the foundations for a healthy life, the role of spontaneous action for health is irreplaceable — for example, social movements, self-help and self-care, encouragement of public participation. There are five key priorities.

● The concept and meaning of 'health promotion' should be clarified at every level of planning, emphasising a social, economic and ecological, rather than a purely physical and mental, perspective on health. Policy development in health promotion has to be integrated with policy in other sectors such as work, housing, social services and primary health care.

● Political commitment to health promotion can be facilitated by the establishment of focal points for health promotion at all levels — local, regional and national. They should provide leadership and accountability so that, when action is agreed, progress will be secured. Adequate funding and skilled personnel are essential to allow the development of intersectoral, coordinated planning in health promotion.

● Continuous consultation, dialogue and exchange of ideas between individuals and groups, both lay and professional, are necessary in order to ensure opportunities for the development of the public interest in health.

- When selecting priority areas for policy development a review should be made of:
  - indicators of health and their distribution in the population
  - current knowledge, skills and health practices of the population
  - current policies in government and other sectors.

  Further, an assessment should be made of:
  - the expected impact on health of different policies and programmes
  - the economic constraints and benefits of different options
  - the social and cultural acceptability of different options
  - the political feasibility of different options.

- Research support is essential for policy development and evaluation to provide a broad understanding of health as well as an assessment of the impact of different initiatives in health promotion. The development of methodologies for research, analysis and evaluation of intervention is essential.

Dilemmas

Health related public policy will always be confronted with basic political and moral dilemmas as it aims to balance public and personal responsibility for health. Some specific conflicts of interest both at the social and the individual levels are:

- The risk of considering health as the ultimate goal, incorporating all life (a kind of 'healthism') with others prescribing what individuals should do for themselves and how they should behave. This is contrary to the principles of health promotion.

- Health promotion programmes inappropriately directed at individuals at the expense of tackling economic and social problems. Policy makers often assume that people have the power completely to shape their own lives so as to be free from the avoidable burden of disease. Thus, when they are ill, they are blamed for this and discriminated against.

- Resources, including information, may not be accessible to people in ways which are sensitive or relevant to their expectations, beliefs, preferences or skills. This may increase social inequalities. Information alone is insufficient; raising awareness without increasing the degree of control or prospects for change may only succeed in generating anxieties and feelings of powerlessness.

- There is a danger that health promotion will be appropriated by one professional group and made a field of specialisation to the exclusion of other professionals and lay people. To increase control over their own health the public require a greater sharing of resources by professionals and government.

These concepts and principles have been well captured by the Ottawa Charter (see diagram) discussed by the participants of the First International Conference on Health Promotion, Ottawa, November 1986. The full text is reproduced in Appendix 3.

OTTAWA CHARTER FOR HEALTH PROMOTION

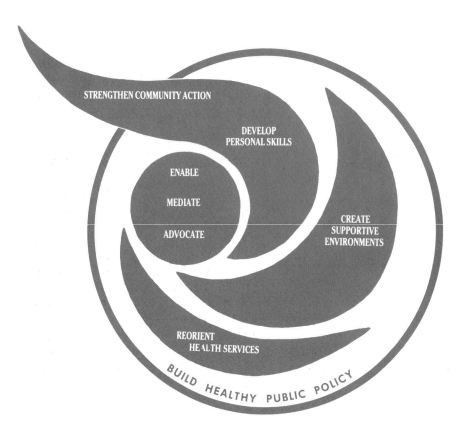

PART ONE

IDENTIFYING THE CHALLENGE

Health Trends and Factors

Good health is a precious resource, not least for elderly people. Now that survival well into our 80s is no longer unusual, a positive approach to health in old age deserves to be promoted vigorously and to shape the attitudes and actions of all sections of our society, from individuals to governments. Mortality rates among older people have been falling, and although this does not inevitably mean that health or morbidity is improving, in the absence of reliable information on the topic, the consensus in Britain seems to be that some modest improvement has taken place.

Worrying, however, is the fact that we are falling behind other countries in the league table. Earlier this century, mortality in the United Kingdom was, in relative terms, among the lowest, but now there are more nations with longer life expectancy at birth (Figure 1). This is an indictment of British society and a principal reason for urging critical examination of our principles and practices over the wide range of activities relevant to health. The improvements of recent years are indicative of what can be done, but the performance of other nations demonstrates that we can do more. From 1961 to 1984 the female mortality rate among those aged 75 to 84 years fell from 87.8 to 61.7 per 1000, or by 30 per cent. At earlier and later ages, and among males, the improvement has not been so impressive but declines of one fifth were characteristic (Office of Population Censuses and Surveys, 1985). The female advantage in late-age mortality has been steadily increasing for at least half a century, although since around 1971 mortality improvements among males aged 55-64 years have been faster than among females. Figure 1 also shows the female advantage in life expectancy at birth in 1982-86 for a number of developed countries. In all of them women, on average, expect to live longer than men. In the United Kingdom the excess is not as high as in countries like the USA or France and although current data suggest that these differences may be narrowing the evidence is not yet conclusive.

FIGURE 1 · LIFE EXPECTANCY IN SELECTED COUNTRIES AT AGE 65 AND AT BIRTH, 1985

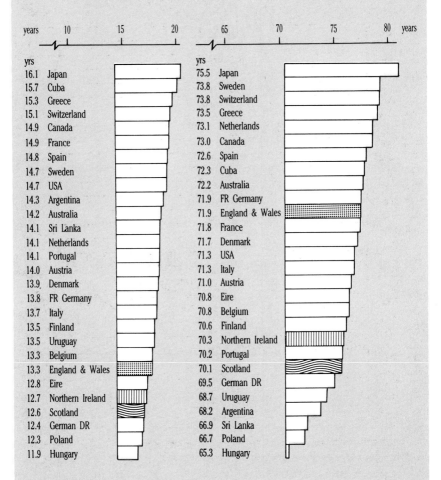

AT AGE 65		MALES	AT BIRTH	
years	10 15 20		65 70 75 80	years
yrs			yrs	
16.1	Japan		75.5	Japan
15.7	Cuba		73.8	Sweden
15.3	Greece		73.8	Switzerland
15.1	Switzerland		73.5	Greece
14.9	Canada		73.1	Netherlands
14.9	France		73.0	Canada
14.8	Spain		72.6	Spain
14.7	Sweden		72.3	Cuba
14.7	USA		72.2	Australia
14.3	Argentina		71.9	FR Germany
14.2	Australia		71.9	England & Wales
14.1	Sri Lanka		71.8	France
14.1	Netherlands		71.7	Denmark
14.1	Portugal		71.3	USA
14.0	Austria		71.3	Italy
13.9	Denmark		71.0	Austria
13.8	FR Germany		70.8	Eire
13.7	Italy		70.8	Belgium
13.5	Finland		70.6	Finland
13.5	Uruguay		70.3	Northern Ireland
13.3	Belgium		70.2	Portugal
13.3	England & Wales		70.1	Scotland
12.8	Eire		69.5	German DR
12.7	Northern Ireland		68.7	Uruguay
12.6	Scotland		68.2	Argentina
12.4	German DR		66.9	Sri Lanka
12.3	Poland		66.7	Poland
11.9	Hungary		65.3	Hungary

AT AGE 65   FEMALES   AT BIRTH

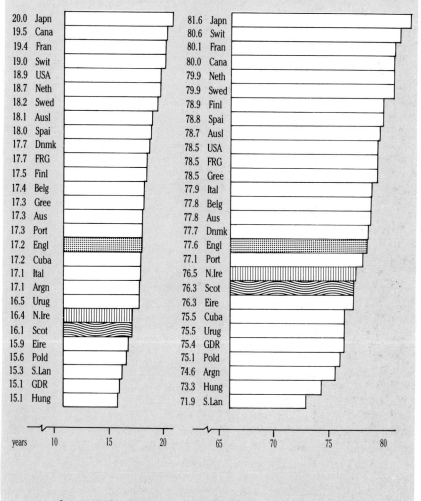

AT AGE 65		AT BIRTH	
20.0	Japn	81.6	Japn
19.5	Cana	80.6	Swit
19.4	Fran	80.1	Fran
19.0	Swit	80.0	Cana
18.9	USA	79.9	Neth
18.7	Neth	79.9	Swed
18.2	Swed	78.9	Finl
18.1	Ausl	78.8	Spai
18.0	Spai	78.7	Ausl
17.7	Dnmk	78.5	USA
17.7	FRG	78.5	FRG
17.5	Finl	78.5	Gree
17.4	Belg	77.9	Ital
17.3	Gree	77.8	Belg
17.3	Aus	77.8	Aus
17.3	Port	77.7	Dnmk
17.2	Engl	77.6	Engl
17.2	Cuba	77.1	Port
17.1	Ital	76.5	N.Ire
17.1	Argn	76.3	Scot
16.5	Urug	76.3	Eire
16.4	N.Ire	75.5	Cuba
16.1	Scot	75.5	Urug
15.9	Eire	75.4	GDR
15.6	Pold	75.1	Pold
15.3	S.Lan	74.6	Argn
15.1	GDR	73.3	Hung
15.1	Hung	71.9	S.Lan

years   10   15   20   65   70   75   80

Source: WHO, *World Health Statistics 1987*, WHO, Geneva, 1987.

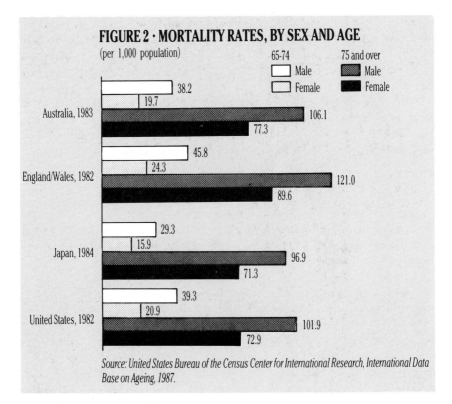

FIGURE 2 · MORTALITY RATES, BY SEX AND AGE

(per 1,000 population)

	65-74	75 and over
	☐ Male	▨ Male
	☐ Female	■ Female

Australia, 1983
- 38.2
- 19.7
- 106.1
- 77.3

England/Wales, 1982
- 45.8
- 24.3
- 121.0
- 89.6

Japan, 1984
- 29.3
- 15.9
- 96.9
- 71.3

United States, 1982
- 39.3
- 20.9
- 101.9
- 72.9

Source: United States Bureau of the Census Center for International Research, International Data Base on Ageing, 1987.

These mortality differentials between the sexes persist in older age groups. In all developed countries, male mortality rates are higher than female rates for both the 'young' and the 'old' elderly. Again the British data compare unfavourably with those from other industrialised countries as shown in Figure 2. In developed countries life expectancy at age 65 is considerably higher for elderly women compared with men. Substantial increases in life expectancy at 65 years of age have occurred for both men and women in most of these countries since the beginning of the century. These gains are still occurring; in fact, at a faster rate than gains in life expectancy at birth. From 1960 to 1980 in the United States for instance, life expectancy at birth increased by 6 per cent while at age 65 it increased by 15 per cent (from 12.8 to 14.1 years among men and from 15.8 to 18.3 years among women). In Sweden recent gains in life expectancy have mainly been achieved through further life expectancy for those over the age 60 (Svanborg, personal communication).

World Health Statistics publishes regularly cohort mortality trends by five year age groups and sex for specific causes of death for a wide range of countries. The first cohort for which data are available is that born in 1899-1900. Therefore, for the age group 60-64 years mortality rates are now available for five cohorts, for that aged 65-69 four cohorts, and for the age group 70-74 three cohorts. The rates for those aged 75 and over are not provided as they are often less reliable.

The analysis of mortality trends for all causes of death considered together for these elderly age groups reveals similar patterns for males and females and for successive five year age groups. These are illustrated by data for females aged 60-64 in Figure 3. The patterns are:

● countries which presented relatively high rates in the past and which show a definite upward trend, particularly for males — for example, Czechoslovakia and Hungary

● countries which exhibited high rates but have experienced a substantial decline over recent years, particularly among females — for example, Finland

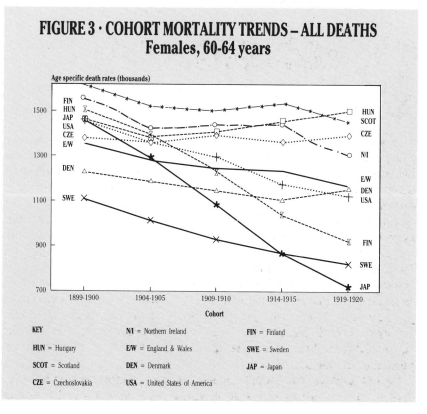

FIGURE 3 · COHORT MORTALITY TRENDS – ALL DEATHS
Females, 60-64 years

KEY

HUN = Hungary

SCOT = Scotland

CZE = Czechoslovakia

N/I = Northern Ireland

E/W = England & Wales

DEN = Denmark

USA = United States of America

FIN = Finland

SWE = Sweden

JAP = Japan

● countries with middle-range rates both in the past and more recently (that is, countries in which elderly people by age groups of both sexes have experienced some but not substantial decreases in mortality rates — for example, England and Wales and the USA)

● countries which enjoyed particularly low mortality rates for elderly people of both sexes in the past but where they have levelled off in the last few years — for example, Sweden and Denmark.

Against this background Japan is a country that stands out for the remarkable decreases in mortality rates for the elderly age groups which have been achieved in the last two or three decades for both sexes. Indeed, for the three age groups considered, both for females and males, Japan exhibits lower mortality rates than any other country. Life expectancy at birth and at the age of 65 for both sexes is higher in Japan than in any other country in the world (Figure 1). Altogether the Japanese figures suggest that a lot can be achieved in terms of improving the mortality experience of elderly people in a very short period of time.

Apart from the fact that international comparisons are not favourable to Britain, there are other good reasons for focusing on the health of older people. Ill health is more likely to occur among them than among younger people, and their families' abilities to assist with its consequences are undermined by low incomes and poor housing of the older age groups.

An active approach to the alleviation of poverty is crucial in this respect. Older people's lives become impoverished in many ways that have a direct impact on their physical and psychological wellbeing. Britain is not doing well here. A recent study comparing six industrial societies provides evidence of a steady increase in mean household income with the age of householders until retirement age but of decline thereafter. This decline is accentuated in some countries and it is actually greater in Britain than in the United States, the Federal Republic of Germany, Norway, Sweden and Canada — the other countries included in the study. The ratio of the adjusted disposable household income of elderly people (75+ years) to the national mean around 1980 was 0.67 in the United Kingdom while in Sweden it was 0.78 (the second lowest) and in the United States 0.84 (the highest). If the 65-74 years age group is used for the comparison, the figure for Britain is 0.76, for Sweden 0.96 and for the United States 0.99. A summary of the findings for Britain, the United States and West Germany is provided in Figure 4. In Great Britain, one quarter of those aged 65-74 years and 40 per cent of those aged 75 years and over had an income lower than half the national median, while the figures for Norway for the same year (1979) were 3 and 9 per cent respectively.

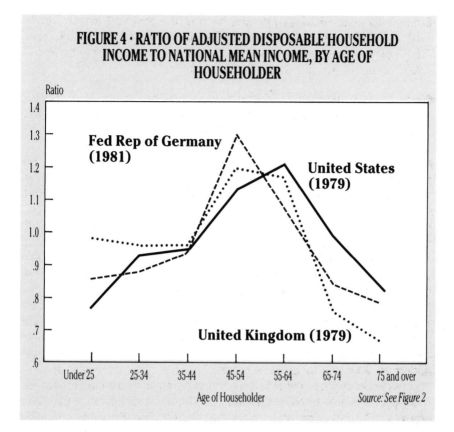

FIGURE 4 · RATIO OF ADJUSTED DISPOSABLE HOUSEHOLD INCOME TO NATIONAL MEAN INCOME, BY AGE OF HOUSEHOLDER

Ratio

Fed Rep of Germany (1981)

United States (1979)

United Kingdom (1979)

Under 25   25-34   35-44   45-54   55-64   65-74   75 and over

Age of Householder

Source: See Figure 2

The assumption that old age is a period in life when 'rest and quietness' are important requisites should not be misused. Above all, there are basic human requirements; young and elderly people alike need to lead interesting and fulfilling lives. The quality of life is inadequately measured by life expectancy expressed as a period of years. A recent study in Canada has compared life expectancy at birth by social class and then by 'quality adjusted life year — QALY'. The first measurement allowed a difference of 2.8 years comparing social classes I (professional and managerial groups) and V (unskilled manual workers) (72.5 and 69.7 years respectively). However, where an adjustment for the 'quality of life' was made, the differential of 6.9 years, from 66.3 to 59.4 years, was much higher.

Pronounced variations exist in the United Kingdom in late age mortality among people of contrasting educational attainment, occupational histories and incomes. Strong variations also persist among the historic nations and provinces of the United Kingdom, and among the official

19

TABLE 1 · DEATH RATES PER 1000 AT AGE 65-74 YEARS FOR MAJOR REGIONS AND NATIONS OF GREAT BRITAIN

	males	females		males	females
Countries			*Regions*		
England	44.0	23.8	North	51.8	28.2
Wales	47.4	24.7	Yorks and Humber	46.3	25.6
Scotland	52.0	28.3	East Midland	43.9	23.7
			East Anglia	39.5	21.5
Metropolitan Counties			South East	41.1	21.8
Greater London	42.8	22.6	South West	41.1	21.8
Greater Manchester	51.1	27.5	West Midland	47.1	24.8
South Yorkshire	46.7	25.0	North West	49.3	27.8
Tyne and Wear	54.1	28.8			
West Midlands	48.6	24.8			
West Yorkshire	47.5	27.4			

Source: Office of Population Censuses and Surveys (1985) 1984 Mortality Statistics. Area, England & Wales, DH5 No 11 HMSO, London, Table 2

regions of England (Table 1). No one disputes the existence of these differentials, but there is debate, in which the media have joined, over whether they have been increasing in recent years (Health Education Council, 1987). Whatever the case, the present social differentials in mortality are greater than they should be: most of the workshop participants believe that they can, and should, be considerably reduced.

This document is a call for action but not from a standing start. During the last decades life expectancy has increased and the standard of living of elderly people has improved. Specialised housing, residential care, and domiciliary services have all expanded from low bases since mid-century. Most recently, we have seen elderly or retired people becoming more active in promoting their own interests and utilising their own resources. This has had diverse manifestations, from the emergence of the 'third age' social movement to the increasing attention paid by commercial interests to elderly people as consumers.

Some positive changes have also been occurring among health professionals. 'Old age' is less and less accepted as an explanation in itself for ill health, and the view is spreading that the common diseases of later life can be treated, cured more often, and in many cases more effectively managed. Professional attitudes towards elderly people are probably changing for the better, and a tendency to regard their problems as of lower priority than those of working age people is probably in decline. There is also some evidence that we have been distancing ourselves from an exclusively 'medicalised' model to one in which there is more willingness to proclaim not only when an elderly person is *ill* but also when he or she is well. Geriatric medicine has developed rapidly in Britain in recent years, clearly demonstrating that appropriate help for elderly people who are ill greatly increases their longer-term health prospects. In general practice medicine and community medicine, much more attention is being devoted to innovations and assessment in treatment and long-term care. Some of these are reported in Part Three.

Positive changes have therefore occurred and the health and wellbeing of elderly people have been improving. One way of making further progress is to accelerate the adoption of the most effective innovations and good practices. A selection of the most highly regarded and successful innovations, as provided by different agencies, individuals and institutions consulted throughout the exercise which led to this report, is therefore included in Part Three.

Another element of the task of health promotion is to broaden the scope of critical examination and action. While the growing relative importance of chronic and disabling conditions in later life as opposed to acute and infectious diseases is well known, and is associated with a decline in the lethal effect of common cardiovascular and cancerous disorders, there is less recognition of the salience of an individual's personal, social and material circumstances in coping with chronic or mild disorders. A condition that creates dependence and loss of self-esteem in one person is coped with successfully, and without prejudice to their autonomy or dignity, in another. The diversity of elderly people in terms of their age, material resources, family support, and competence is vast. But many are vulnerable to the disabling effects of dysfunction, or to the loss of support from spouses, relatives or carers.

Studies of the situation of elderly people in Britain frequently emphasise the importance to individuals of such qualities as autonomy, morale, independence and self-esteem, and the relationship of these to states of health. For each elderly person there is interdependence between material wellbeing, their household and housing situation, and their satisfaction with their personal situation and health. An increase in the degree of interdependence and autonomy among elderly people is likely to be associated with a significant improvement in their health.

In this wider view, health is inextricably linked on the one hand to an individual's personal circumstances and on the other to the country's socio-economic structure and health care system. We believe that to maximise improvements in the health of elderly people, a more comprehensive approach to policy and practice than that concerned only with medical and social services should be adopted. More and closer liaison between the disparate agencies involved with elderly people should be fostered, perhaps under the umbrella of local or regional coordinators. All too often, essential contributors — such as housing, the voluntary sector and the media — are left out or marginalised.

Even such fundamental structural arrangements as the life time distribution of income become relevant to a comprehensive consideration of health factors, and in some of our discussions the relevance to health of, for example, public policies in the field of housing investment was stressed. But if there is a consensus pointing to the need to embrace a wider field of action, it is not so clear how far to widen the area of concern.

The Scope of Health Promotion in Old Age

As early as 1948 the World Health Organization declared that health is 'a complete state of physical, mental and social wellbeing'. While this statement encapsulates our view that there is more to health than combating dysfunction and disorders, the agenda for action that it sets is potentially infinite. The ultimate objective of promoting a 'healthier old age' is inevitably the concern of the whole of society and has to start early in life, with an emphasis on dietary, environmental and behavioural measures. However, we believe that much can be done to improve the health of those who have already reached old age. A broad view of the factors which must be tackled to improve health implies diverse action including legislative and fiscal measures in the fields of income support, social services, housing and transport. However, the course of health promotion might itself be diluted if the focus of a campaign were too broadly set. Professionals, politicians and polemicists are likely to differ on the extent to which the factors of material, social and emotional wellbeing can be tackled, and on the means to be adopted.

We therefore felt there was much merit in the set of recommendations produced in 1986 in the Ottawa Charter for Health Promotion which moved some way beyond disease prevention and treatment (see Introduction and Appendix 3). The Charter argued that each country should:

● build public policies for health at both national and local levels

● strengthen community action

● reorient health services towards the pursuit of health

● develop personal skills by providing appropriate information and education.

This begins to specify the scope of health promotion. Even so, the recommendations are loosely defined, and if practical measures are to be adopted, more specific recommendations relevant to the United Kingdom are needed. The task is to strike a balance between highlighting the main impediments to improved health with a view to their removal, and the practical goal of generating and putting into operation new ways of reaching feasible targets.

When setting the tasks for our meetings and consultations we did not aim to define a policy agenda or establish priorities. Instead, we recommend that organisations and individuals set targets specific to their own responsibilities and consider ways in which they might collaborate, for example, by locality/patch planning.

Key Assumptions about Health in Old Age

Few of the principles and assumptions in this document are based on tested propositions for in many cases there is no available evidence. Research has not yet established beyond doubt the causes of ill health or the ways of preventing it. Some of the hypotheses imply a long interval between cause and effect, others suggest a multiplicity of interacting causal factors and are therefore exceptionally difficult to test empirically. The following six assumptions, or hypotheses, concerning the fundamental and long-term factors which influence health attracted broad support from the participants in the discussions: *conclusion*

- Old age is not a disease but a normal stage of life.

- Most people of 60 years and over are fit and healthy, but as they age they become less capable of recovering quickly, or completely, from illness and are more likely to become frail and in need of help to maintain their capacity for self care.

- Functional capacity in old age can be strengthened through training/ stimulation and/or by avoiding factors associated with ill health.

- Elderly people are more diverse socially and psychologically than young people, reflecting the fact that they have been exposed for a longer time to life-long risks and to varied life experiences. These are reflected in a wide variety of beliefs, values and needs.

- The promotion of health in old age should be directed towards the promotion of good mental, physical and social function as well as to the prevention of disease and disability.

● Many measures which affect the health of elderly people lie beyond the formal health sector. Health and social welfare personnel are, however, well placed to act as advocates for change outside, as well as inside, their own direct sphere of work.

The Knowledge that is Lacking in Britain

A longitudinal perspective is invaluable when discussing health in old age. It is only by adopting such an approach that a distinction between the manifestations of ageing and the effects of definable diseases is made possible. Unfortunately, no longitudinal studies have been set up yet in Britain with the specific objective of recording the varied manifestations and correlates of increasing age. We have to borrow from the knowledge generated by studies in other countries. This is by definition unsatisfactory: one of the main conclusions of such studies is that there are important differences from one cohort to another even in countries with ethnically homogeneous populations and within a short period of years from each other.

Perhaps the most comprehensive longitudinal study on old age is that of the 70 year olds in Gotenburg, Sweden (Svanborg, 1988). It incorporates a broad, multidimensional investigation covering many of the basic biological, clinical, behavioural and social perspectives provided by age-related morphological, biochemical, physiological and psychological changes. It has now looked at three cohorts. The first (born 1901-1902) has been followed for 15 years, the second cohort (1906-1907) for nine, and to the third (born 1911-1912) an intervention dimension was added to the original protocol. The individuals included in the study have been shown to be representative of the total population which is fairly stable and homogeneous. Therefore, the findings cannot be attributed either to migration or to genetic changes.

Some remarkable differences have been found where the first two cohorts were compared, both in terms of rate and manifestations of ageing. These differences were also quite evident in the comparison between the second and third cohorts. The intervention component added to the last cohort will bring a new dimension to the study and preliminary results are expected within two years. The main aim of such an intervention programme is to establish possible measures for postponing or preventing age-related changes by:

● early and more correct diagnosis and treatment

● improved options for meaningful lives with a reasonable degree of activity

● improved possibilities for preventing or postponing the influence of various risk factors.

The sample in which the interventions were made will be compared with controls of the same cohort, as well as with the 75 year olds from the two previously investigated, longitudinally followed age cohorts. The results from the longitudinal studies are gradually replacing previously held stereotyped and simplified concepts about human ageing. They are therefore very important in setting criteria and providing base line indicators to be used when evaluating interventions. Take for instance the problems related to over- and/or under-diagnosis. Both have been shown to be rather common in the Gotenburg study, over-diagnosis in particular. In discussing the reasons, the leaders of the study argue that it is mainly due to the limited knowledge of how to distinguish the manifestations of psychological ageing from symptoms of definable diseases. One example concerns the diagnosis of hypertensive diseases. The Gotenburg study has shown that the heart volume increases with age, apparently for physiological reasons; such an increase is mainly eccentric (that is, an increased volume due to structural adaptation) while the hypertrophy caused by hypertensive disease is concentric (indicating that the ratio between the volume and thickness of the heart is altered).

The study has also helped to show that 'higher' blood pressure is not necessarily associated with disease in old age. In addition, the Gotenburg study has well documented age-cohort differences in blood pressure, with a statistically significant decrease comparing cohorts 1, 2 and 3 (from 96 to 84 years). In other words, even with the small five-year intervals considered, different cohorts of 70 year olds within this homogeneous population show important differences in their blood pressures: what might have been considered 'low' ten years ago would be relatively 'high' now. The practical result of all of this is that the large number of misdiagnosed 'hypertension patients' are exposed to the iatrogenic effects of, often, very powerful drugs. Only by conducting representative longitudinal studies can knowledge such as this be gained. These should incorporate a wide range of behavioural and social variables. They are long overdue in this country.

Health in Old Age: the Diversity of Challenges

To bring about significant improvements in the health of the older population, interlinked but distinguishable goals can be defined. One short-term objective is to raise the general standard of health; a second is to reduce the prevalence and severity of common disorders and health problems. Improvements in the health of today's elderly population are sought as well as the best possible health for elderly people in the future. The health of Britain's elderly population will be better if there are improvements in nutrition, improvements in housing (including, particularly, higher standards of home heating and insulation), a decline in smoking and in excessive alcohol consumption, and more active participation in modest exercise. It would also improve if medications were more carefully and selectively prescribed and monitored, and the prevalence of iatrogenic diseases reduced. There also needs to be more effective procedures for case finding and early diagnosis of preventable disease where intervention can prevent complication or chronicity.

For significant health improvements in the longer term, there must be a substantial reduction in the incidence of poverty at all ages, but especially among widows, those living alone and the very old. Income-related problems of poor housing, deficient heating and poor diet among the most disadvantaged groups are not only associated with the prevalence of disease, dysfunction and mortality but also with a person's ability to cope with ill health. While our society has virtually eliminated total indigence among elderly people, it still sustains severe poverty and disadvantage among a substantial minority. The government's responsibility in the income field is both to promote the general prosperity of the older population and to raise and strengthen the safety net for the worst off. The former can be tackled both through its own disbursements and by the framework and encouragement that the government sets for private saving and pensions; the latter by more generous transfer payments to widows without independent records of National Insurance contributions or private pensions, to those with disabilities and special housing needs, and to those with deficient housing standards.

A different, but equally demanding, agenda faces biomedical researchers and practitioners, for enormous strides in health could result from advances in our understanding of the aetiology and treatment of arthritis, cancers, cardiovascular disorders, dementias and other common or severe disorders. Not only the quality of life, but also the physical and mental health of those affected by these diseases as well as their carers, will be related to the will and determination of the government, the health and social care professions and the private and voluntary sectors to develop improved nursing, residential and domiciliary services and support to carers.

Part One has attempted to distil and to represent fairly the views which were most forcefully expressed and widely supported during the workshops. Enough have been set down to demonstrate the complexity of factors in our health: not only must we understand the relative importance of, and interactions among, many kinds of influence — individual and societal, behavioural and environmental, material and spiritual — but we also need to unravel circumstances of the present and the past. There are profound problems of understanding, but more than this, and before major advances in our knowledge of health factors are achieved, we have first to address our priorities for action. Through the appraisal of innovative initiatives we can discover where our scarce resources are best deployed to bring about improvements in health. Part Two attempts to represent the scope for action that the workshops saw as the next phase of development in both policy and practice.

References

Health Education Council (1987) *The Health Divide*. London, HEC.

Office of Population Censuses and Surveys (1985) *Population Trends*, No 45, Table 20. London, OPCS.

Svanborg A (1988) The Health of the Elderly Population: Results from Longitudinal Studies with Age-Cohort Comparison. In: *Research and the Ageing Population*. CIBA Foundation, Collection 134, John Wiley & Sons, pp 3-17.

PART TWO

MEETING THE
CHALLENGE

Meeting the challenge identified in Part One requires concerted action from a wide variety of individuals and agencies at three levels:

● **By individuals:**
— self-care among older people themselves
— informal care (families, relatives, friends, neighbours)
— formal care (professional service providers, volunteers)

● **By local agencies:**
(focus on practice)
— local authorities (including housing, education, social services, transport)
— health authorities, family practitioner committees (FPCs)
— voluntary bodies

● **By national agencies:**
(focus on planning and financing)
— central government departments
— appointed bodies
— voluntary agencies
— private sector organisations

The following pages offer suggestions for initiatives and activities that will aid the development of a positive health strategy. Examples of recent initiatives in interprofessional and interagency cooperation in health promotion are given in Part Three. We have not sought to be exhaustive in our coverage but have tried to include examples from various sectors to show what is possible.

Our agenda for policy and action requires a partnership both within and between the three levels mentioned above. We have isolated each level for the purpose of discussion, but in practice they interact. Their various responsibilities can either constrict or expand the range of choices available to older people.

INDIVIDUAL LEVEL

In order to promote a positive image of health and a sense of wellbeing rather than a state of dependence, sickness and passivity, our starting point is the primacy of the individual in his or her health. We do not subscribe to the notion of 'victim blaming' but it is vital to acknowledge the positive contribution that individuals themselves can make to the promotion of their own health. To counteract the tendency to blame people for their own ill-advised habits, we must remember the social and material circumstances which prevailed in their, and their parents', youth. It is not many decades since the consumption of sugar was strongly promoted in the UK, or since the armed services tacitly encouraged smoking among conscripts. Greater participation by older people is vital. Moreover, it can be achieved in a variety of modest ways at minimal cost. Indeed, older people represent a valuable resource which, if released, can do more to promote health than more costly formal services. Examples are given in Part Three.

Self-Care

Increasingly, information is becoming available about what constitutes good physical and mental health. Very often elderly people have either not heard about it, understood it, accepted it or acted upon it. Yet a recent study by the Policy Studies Institute (PSI) shows that providing the right kinds of information in the right way to elderly people can help support them at home and make an important contribution to their health and sense of wellbeing (Tester and Meredith, 1987). The project found that face to face contact was the most effective method in encouraging elderly people to maximise their use of health and welfare services.

If older people could obtain and profit from particular kinds of information, they could enhance their self-care, increase their active involvement in decision-making, and have a greater impact on service provision and policy-making. Organisations like the Citizens Advice Bureaux, pensioners' groups, and the Beth Johnson Foundation all share the aim of making more accessible the information and advice needed by elderly people to take self-care measures.

Health professionals have a particular role in encouraging elderly people to take responsibility for their own wellbeing. The authors of the PSI study mentioned above make it clear that although information-givers need not be professionals, it is essential that they have training in assessing and meeting the information needs of elderly people, and support in updating their information resources. More one to one contact is preferable to the use of the mass media.

Self-care in the elderly population is important in another sense. The majority of elderly people are retired but are also active, fit and energetic. They represent not only the majority of carers of elderly people but also a huge potential resource for disseminating advice, stimulation, and practical help. Promotion of self-care will help raise the status of older people as well as improve their independence, self-esteem and morale. For every identified voluntary group that is helping with transport, shopping or home mainte-nance, there are probably several other unrecognised associations with the same willingness to provide or exchange assistance.

In the United Kingdom we have only just begun to elaborate effective ways of assisting mutual and spontaneous support and care among elderly people. Community care workers can help promote self-help initiatives and various examples exist of community-based projects. We cite some of these in Part Three.

Informal Care

Community care in practice very often means care not by the *community* but by a single, and usually related, individual (normally a spouse or daughter). Such carers frequently and at critical stages certainly require support and relief in their caring. Too often community services are withheld, or withdrawn, if a female carer is present. Support needs to be flexible and geared to the individual needs of carers. This is especially important when growing numbers of carers are themselves elderly. The Disabled Persons (Services, Consultation and Representation) Act 1986 attempted to recog-nise the problems facing carers so that their needs would be assessed if necessary as well as those of the person being cared for. Much of the Act remains to be implemented.

At issue is the health of both the frail person and his or her carer. A great many experiments have taken place in recent years to increase collaboration between informal and formal sources of support and care, including the development of respite care to assist the carers of severely disabled elderly people. It is particularly important for the most successful and cost effective innovations to be diffused and well supported by staff resources and training.

People are no less willing than formerly to care for or support their husbands, wives, parents or other relatives. Nor is there a large untapped pool of informal carers. Community care services do not normally substitute for family or informal care however effective they may be during moments of crisis. We have only just begun in the United Kingdom to address these issues at a national level and a strong case can be made for a more vigorous, explicit statement of policy as called for in Sir Roy Griffiths' agenda for community care (Griffiths, 1988). As numerous commentaries on the slow and uneven implementation of community care as a substitute for long-term institutional care have underlined, more effective use of existing and/or additional resources and better coordinated services are required to develop local facilities and employ staff to enable elderly people to stay in their own homes.

At the same time, it is not only elderly people who require practical information. Carers also need information about what the caring task entails and about what support (both cash and services) is available. Numerous guides are available which set out to provide clearly and simply the information carers might require or find helpful both to manage the caring task and to seek further assistance or advice. There is also scope for a carers' charter to establish more explicitly the nature and extent of their contribution and responsibilities. Such a charter is in preparation at the Informal Caring Support Unit based at the King's Fund Centre.

Formal Care

Attitudes to older people, and to ageing generally, can influence profession-al carers' responses to them. Negative images and stereotypes need to be challenged. Professional development in relation to elderly people may be required to achieve a shift to more positive approaches to health. Professionals might ideally be seen as co-learners rather than as 'experts'. They possess resources to offer older people rather than to do things for them. Practice guidelines could assist in sensitising professionals to these issues. A possible model is *Meeting the Needs of Older People: Some Guidelines* produced by Age Concern England (1986). There are many well women clinics around the country. Is there a case for a similar development in well elderly clinics? Examples of community-based projects in which professionals have become involved are given in Part Three.

Poss conclusion .

LOCAL LEVEL

Health promotion for elderly people, or indeed any group, carries with it implications for the impact of a wide range of policies and services on health. At a local level a number of linkages in policy and organisation require to be established. In local government, for example, there are issues of interdepartmental links between education and social services; of links among local authorities, that is, between counties (regions in Scotland) and districts particularly in relation to housing and leisure; and of links between local authorities and other agencies notably health authorities.

Local Government

Local authorities might be encouraged to undertake health education programmes under the auspices of their domiciliary services such as home carers. Strategic plans for health promotion could be jointly established between social services departments and health authorities. An example of such an initiative is Maidstone Health Authority and Kent Social Services Department's venture on primary prevention which includes nutrition and dietetic advice, no-smoking programmes, foot care programmes, accident prevention and pre-retirement programmes.

Training programmes might be set in motion for all local government staff, including environmental health and housing officers, with the primary purpose of demonstrating how their work impinges on the health of older people. Health promotion officers might be involved in such training. The proposed new Certificate of Social Service course for social workers fundamentally changes the role of social work in the community. This is a positive development which is to be welcomed and it carries with it implications for health promotion and older people.

Education can be separated into continuing education and education for the 'third age'. School curricula could reflect more positive attitudes to older people. In addition to pre-retirement programmes, attention might be given to a 'token system' to enable retired people to buy at any time in the future (when they chose to do so) a range of activities they might wish to undertake.

All planning and building permissions ought wherever possible to reflect their relevance to older people — for example, bus routes, house design, access, lighting and leisure facilities.

Health Authorities (including Primary Health Care)

There is a case for a change from a predominantly demand-led reactive service to one centred on a genuine commitment to health promotion. The White Paper on Primary Health Care's frequent references to promoting better health is encouraging. Elderly people are singled out for special mention but true health promotion is about much more than simply improved screening. More generally, the introduction of general management into the National Health Service was designed to make health authorities more attentive to consumer preferences. The danger is that because general managers are on short-term contracts they will concentrate on matters of pressing importance to the exclusion of less urgent and longer term issues. Moreover, consumerism ought to be about more than superficial exercises in image-creation.

A shift towards health promotion is being contemplated at a time when a number of policy changes are in the air. As well as the primary health care proposals there is the development of neighbourhood nursing, the future of nursing training and Project 2000 is under discussion, and the Griffiths review of community care in England and Wales which proposes a lead agency role for social services departments in the development of community care. If accepted this will have profound, although as yet unclear, implications for health authorities' involvement in community care. In addition, an interest in standards of care (for example, the Royal College of General Practitioners' quality initiative) is likely to lead to specific statements about the primary care of elderly people including a commitment to health promotion.

The climate of change we are witnessing in a variety of spheres offers real opportunities to examine critically existing services and their future development. It also affords the opportunity for more experimentation and innovation than has been customary in health and social services. As a major employer, the NHS has an important example to set with respect to its own policies and attitudes to the promotion of health.

Priority areas for consideration include the following:

Participation/Representation

Community health councils and, where they exist, patient participation groups provide feedback about services to users but attention is also needed at authority, managerial and delivery levels to secure more active consumer input which is constructive as well as critical. There are, for instance, examples of elderly forums which offer a channel of communication between users and services (see Part Three). The need for independent advocates to assist individuals and their carers requiring support merits further exploration and experimentation.

Organisation and Management

Health authorities are responsible for developing policies on health promotion. Existing mechanisms for performance review between the DHSS and regional health authorities might be used to ensure that health-related targets are included among those on which general managers' performance is assessed. Such targets should relate to health rather than to finance.

The action of some health authorities in appointing managers specifically to run services for elderly people is welcomed provided that the structure of the authority actually permits the development of a comprehensive service for this age group and not merely a sickness service.

Patch/neighbourhood models of primary care, and of health and social care more generally, create the potential for more accurately targeted resources at the delivery level. They also increase the potential for local consumer input and a further expansion of teamwork. The Kent Community Care Project for frail elderly people, primarily a social services model, may have important lessons for the organisation of community health (including primary care) services at local level; two such lessons are the key worker or case manager concept, and the provision of delegated budgets to these individuals which allows them to put together appropriate services to maintain clients in their own homes.

Given the vital role performed by general practitioners (GPs) and other members of the primary care team, family practitioner committees (FPCs) ought to be more actively involved in policy development in regard to health promotion for elderly people. The White Paper gives encouragement to this objective. FPCs do not exist in Scotland where general practitioner services are more closely allied to health authorities. In principle, this allows GPs and others in primary care, such as community nurses, to become more readily involved in health promotion. Whether they do so or not may merit further inquiry.

Resources

Health authorities' earmarked budgets for health promotion need to be more specifically identified. While additional resources are needed, it is equally important to identify more creative ways of using existing staff and budgets for health promotion. Examples of new initiatives which do not involve additional resources are given in Part Three.

Research and Evaluation

All of the above needs to be evaluated on a continuing basis. Local policy and practice can only benefit from a more informed base of epidemiological and sociological knowledge. A national research strategy for health promotion therefore needs to be developed and supported (see next section). In addition, there is a need for more systematic evaluation of innovative schemes to aid policy and organisational learning.

Training/Education

Growing support for multidisciplinary care among service providers is welcomed but more attention needs to be given in the curricula to the inclusion of health promotion, attitudes to older people, and anticipatory care as well as disease avoidance. There is a need to replace a medical model approach to health promotion with a holistic, person-centred model.

Voluntary Sector

Increasingly, the voluntary sector performs an indirect role in health promotion alongside the statutory services. Coordinated joint planning requires sustained input from this sector as has been recognised, for example, by the National Council of Voluntary Organisations. Voluntary agencies are also an important source of innovation and new ways of providing support from which mainstream services can learn.

NATIONAL LEVEL

Nationally there exists a diverse range of agencies and interests whose activities impinge either directly or indirectly on the health of elderly people. They include central government; national bodies like the Sports Council, the Scottish Community Education Council, and many others; research councils; the media; the Health Education Authority and its counterparts elsewhere in the UK; and inspectorates or advisory bodies such as the Social Services Inspectorate (SSI) and the Health Advisory Service (HAS).

One task of national level governmental or quasi-governmental institutions is to promote research, to disseminate its findings, and to encourage/facilitate local initiatives and action. As we noted in Part One, there are extensive gaps in our knowledge of ageing. In particular, there is a need for longitudinal studies on morbidity to provide essential information on causes of disability among older people and the coping mechanisms deployed to cope with life events such as bereavement. We know too little about the 'well elderly' as opposed to the 'problematic elderly'. The DHSS's Chief Scientist, the Medical Research Council and the Economic and Social Research Council, among other research bodies, should give their coordinated attention to this topic.

There is a need, too, for strengthened links between central government departments. This was recognised over a decade ago by the former 'think tank', the Central Policy Review Staff, in an influential report, *A Joint Framework for Social Policies* (Central Policy Review Staff, 1975). A strategic forum for Ministers was proposed which would provide an opportunity to consider policy concerns which went beyond the boundaries of any single department. The initiative proved to be short-lived, largely because of the absence of political will.

The Department of Health (DoH) cannot be held solely responsible for initiatives designed to promote health but it might consider making it its business to put health promotion and ageing on to the agendas of other departments and agencies in the fields of transport, education, environment and housing to ensure that policy initiatives do not run counter to the notion of positive health. Perhaps the concept of health impact statements, akin to environmental impact statements, merits attention. The Acheson report on the future of public health medicine recommends the creation of a small unit within the DoH to monitor policies for their impact on health. This proposal has been accepted by Ministers.

The private sector also has an important role to perform both in providing services, such as home nurses, and in participating in public campaigns. For example, the campaign Heartbeat Wales owes much of its considerable success to liaison between the Welsh Office and Tesco plc.

There is surely scope for further sponsorship of this kind.

There needs to be continuous evaluation of progress against agreed targets. Bodies like the SSI and HAS can assist in this process by producing inter-authority comparisons, and by spreading good practice among local agencies. This is also a role for national voluntary bodies which is already performed to some extent by the Volunteer Centre.

The media have a responsibility for promoting health among older people both nationally and locally. Apart from presenting a more positive image of ageing, television might be used to perform simple health tests such as eye testing, memory testing and so on thereby aiding self-care. Furthermore, simple exercises could be offered to older people through the medium of television, and information could be provided on matters such as nutrition and diet. The royal colleges and national training bodies might consider devoting some of their attention to the needs of professionals for training in health promotion among older people.

References

Age Concern England (1986) *Meeting the Needs of Older People: Some Practice Guidelines.* Mitcham, Surrey, Age Concern.

Central Policy Review Staff (1975) *A Joint Framework for Social Policies.* London, HMSO.

R Griffiths (1988) *Community Care: Agenda for Action.* London, HMSO.

S Tester and B Meredith (1987) *Ill-informed?* London, Policy Studies Institute.

PART THREE

INNOVATIONS IN PRACTICE

At the first workshop it was agreed to collect details of recent innovations in the delivery of information and advice about health in later life, and about new approaches to the management in the community of health problems. This final section of our report is a list of these initiatives. The focus is on experimental and new ideas and not on those innovations in services which have been widely adopted as 'good practice': such initiatives are well described in national reviews of social services, social work and of community and hospital medical services (Andrews and Brocklehurst, 1987; British Medical Association, 1986; Department of Health and Social Security, 1987; Means and Smith, 1985; Sinclair, 1988).

Our list is not comprehensive, nor can we claim that all the ideas to which it refers have been evaluated or will be the most cost-effective, influential or successful. We have been able to do little more than sample the range of constructive and creative ideas which can be seen in Britain today. They demonstrate what is possible and offer a glimpse of the varied activities around the country. We believe that the next step is a series of evaluative research studies, the results of which would encourage the dissemination and replication of successful schemes.

Good ideas require recognition and approval before they are adopted by others. Gaining approval is a complex process in the field of health promotion among elderly people. It is difficult to reach a firm conclusion about the comparative advantages of particular innovations because often:

● there is a long interval between the intervention and the outcome

● the benefits are often in terms of the comfort, gains in healthy years or quality of life of people, and the mixture of quantitative and qualitative outcomes is extremely difficult to assess consistently and as a whole

● many innovations focus on changed and collaborative responsibilities among staff from different organisations and agencies, making them unusually difficult to cost and assess for their administrative practicality

● existing routine sources of information on the health of the British population are patchy and poor; the data base with which to monitor health improvements rarely exists.

As in many other fields, often the scarcity is not of good ideas but of funds, staff, or innovators — people willing and able to act as agents of change. Another handicap is that the best indicative methods and practice of project evaluation are infrequently employed. As the Team for Elderly People at St Mary Abbott's Hospital, Chelsea, has stated, 'traditional quantitative evaluation techniques are often not appropriate but are demanded by managers who have little understanding of other methods . . . . It is essential that professionals are given appropriate training in evaluating their work.' Researchers in the field are still improving the methods of measuring the benefits to individuals or the cost effectiveness of any proposal. Some proposed approaches, such as the use of quality of life measures, remain controversial. Cost-benefit analyses incorporating even the principal non-pecuniary benefits of an innovation are out of fashion. The merits of alternative investments or deployments of staff time are rarely assessed, and few studies consider the opportunity costs of a service development. These are however the very issues that have to be weighed by the managers of service programmes, from curriculum planners in social work, and those developing the 'business plans' of health authorities, to those running a sports centre or an adult education institute. The immediate needs are for better liaison between managers, budget controllers and innovators, and for the wider adoption of evaluation methods which are relatively straightforward but have a consumer orientation.

To apply sophisticated and comprehensive evaluation methods to every innovation would itself be a diversion of resources, but a middle way that examines more than the direct cost to a service providing agency is needed to identify the most effective approaches to health promotion. While the problem of allocating scarce resources is always present, some schemes and reforms have been shown to have important benefits for elderly people and on any grounds should be adopted more widely. It is also the case that we do not always understand why some health promotion measures work when others fail to have obvious impact. As one example, we do not know why some campaigns in health education succeed, as with the wide public understanding of the benefits from reducing saturated-fats consumption, while others appear to be crying into the wind.

No one has suggested that we are yet at the stage where innovations are too common: the problems are more that there are inadequate mechanisms either to differentiate the excellent from the worthy, or to diffuse the best ideas and encourage their adoption. One member of the workshop put the situation well: 'while we have been able neither to set precise objectives for health in old age, nor to develop a strategy for action, there has been unanimous support for promoting good practice. There must be an interim stage, during which it would be valuable to develop a resource book for a wide audience at each level of action and responsibility'. This part of our document is a first step in this direction.

The following pages list recent innovations which have been brought to our attention. It partially updates recent reviews of the field (Isaacs and Evers, 1984). A brief description of each scheme or project is given together with contact addresses for further details. In some instances a fuller published account is referenced and the details will be found in the list of references at the end of this chapter. As far as possible the order of the topics is that used in Part Two of this report.

INDIVIDUAL SELF-CARE AND PREVENTIVE APPROACHES

Self-Care: General

Several organisations and individuals have for some time been exploring various approaches to health education and promotion among elderly people. Often the reports of the effectiveness of these initiatives are positive but a general problem seems to be the lack of both funding and organisational support with which to diffuse the ideas and to reach a larger population. Several organisations have been particularly active and now have a considerable depth of experience and insight into the practical problems of out-reach programmes. An interesting recent study has shown the extent to which elderly people living in an urban setting are informed about the agencies, services and sources of advice available in the health promotion and other fields (Tester and Meredith, 1987).

Contact addresses:
- Age Concern England, Bernard Sunley House, 60 Pitcairn Road, Mitcham, Surrey CR4 3LL (tel: 01 640 5431)

- Age Concern Scotland, 33 Castle Street, Edinburgh EH2 3DN (tel: 031 225 5000)

- Alzheimer's Disease Society, Bank Lodges, Fulham Broadway, London SW6 1EP (tel: 01 381 3177)

- Beth Johnson Foundation, Parkside House, 64 Princes Road, Hartshill, Stoke on Trent ST4 7JL (tel: 0782 44030)

- British Association for Service to the Elderly, 3 Keele Farmhouse, Keele, Staffordshire ST5 5AR (tel: 0782 627280)

- Centre for Health and Retirement Education, Centre for Extra-Mural Studies, 26 Russell Square, London WC1B 5DQ (tel: 01 636 8000 ext 3873)

- Health Education Authority, Hamilton House, Mabledon Place, London WC1H 9TX (tel: 01 631 0930)

- Help the Aged, St James's Walk, London EC1R OBE (tel: 01 608 2693)

- Scottish Community Education Council, Atholl House, 2 Canning Street, Edinburgh, EH3 8EG (tel: 031 229 2433)

- Scottish Health Education Group, Dorothy Walster, Woodburn House, Canaan Lane, Edinburgh EH10 4SG (tel: 031 447 8044)

Health Advice: Literature, Shops, Courses, Campaigns

The Health Education Authority (formerly Council) in 1985 established a five year programme, *Health in Old Age*, to encourage a positive approach to health in old age, primarily through the dissemination of the results of existing initiatives with an emphasis on good practice. An important part of the programme has been *Age Well*, a nationwide campaign based with Age Concern England. It has concentrated on motivating older people, health professionals and community organisations to initiate and to expand their work concerned with health in later life, through *Age Well* shows around the country, study days and workshops.

The HEA also funds the Centre for Health and Retirement Education at the Centre for Extra-Mural Studies in the University of London. It has a national remit to develop training programmes for health educators and has inaugurated a new Diploma in Mid- and Later-Life Planning. The Centre has developed the ideas pack, *Health and Retirement: Ideas and Resources for Health Educators*. This pack is for anyone involved in running a session or course on health for people who are about to retire. It contains a folder with ten units of ideas about learning and teaching, twenty items for use in health sessions and a video cassette with four trigger films to start discussion.

Although the HEA's elderly programme is now secondary to its AIDS responsibilities, the Centre continues the work of developing, disseminating and evaluating a range of information packs and educational materials for people in middle and later life. Most recently it has produced a 16 page booklet, *What Next? Focus on Health*, for those in their 50s about improving and maintaining their health.

Another HEA initiative has been the Look After Yourself campaign which began in 1980. It uses HEA trained tutors to run courses throughout the country. LAY courses create awareness about how lifestyle affects health. One scheme, developed in collaboration with Age Concern

Leicester, was offered to elderly people in the town in June 1987. Tutors were employed by Leicestershire Health Authority and premises were provided by Age Concern. The course includes materials on diet, exercise, stress control, alcohol, smoking, relaxation and social health, and there are options on weight control, the use of prescribed medicines, and common minor ailments. It has been very well received. It has just (1988) been announced in the Centre's (free) newsletter that a register is to be created of approved HEA trainers and tutors, each of whom will have received special training.

Contact address: *See above*

Initiatives have been taken by other bodies on spreading information and advice on the improvement and maintenance of health in later life. These range from the Senior Health Shop established by the Beth Johnson Foundation in Hanley, Stoke on Trent, to the organisation of health days and fairs in many parts of the country — for example, Greenwich (Cloke and Payne, 1985), Tower Hamlets, West Lambeth, Southwark and Aberdeen. In the London Borough of Hammersmith and Fulham, collaboration between the local Age Concern Group, the Social Services Department and the Bishop Creighton House Settlement led to annual 'Health and Fun Festivals' (London Borough of Hammersmith and Fulham, 1987). The same group are involved with the provision of a health course for older women. The Scottish Health Education Group has supported a 50+ Health Information Project in the Easterhouse district of Glasgow. A wide range of activities continues, from keep-fit and swimming groups to an 'elderly-care' service. Help the Aged (1988) has published a practical health handbook for older people.

Contact address: *See above*

Well Elderly Clinics

There is currently great interest and debate among the medical profession and elsewhere about the potential role of 'well elderly' clinics as a setting for both the dissemination of health education and as a venue for preventive medicine. Several schemes have been operating for many years, and their role in case finding and early diagnosis is recognised (Freer, 1985; Kinnaird and others, 1981; Kennie, 1986; Taylor and others, 1983; Vetter and others, 1984).

Among more recent innovations, the Team for Elderly People at St Mary Abbott's Hospital, Chelsea, has established a health assessment and an advisory service for any person of at least 55 years of age. The team includes a health visitor, dietitian, chiropodist, occupational therapist, speech therapist and physiotherapist. No specific medical procedures are undertaken, rather the health of the individual is examined in the context of their social situation. Health problems related to daily functioning are tackled rather than their symptoms: if symptoms require medical treatment a person is referred to their general practitioner and referrals are made to other agencies if necessary. As well as offering individual appointments the Team has developed health sessions for groups of well elderly and they hope to develop a peer health counselling scheme based on the Beth Johnson Foundation project. There has been a pilot scheme attempting to find those housebound elderly individuals who may be more 'at risk'. Another well elderly clinic has been operating for many years in Bolton.

Contact addresses:

- Team for Elderly People, St Mary Abbott's Hospital, Marloes Road, London W8 (tel: 01 937 8181)

- Dr Arup Banerjee, Dept of Geriatric Medicine, Bolton General Hospital, Minerva Road, Bolton, Lancs BL4 OJS

Self-Care: Nutrition, Smoking, Exercise and Fitness

The Gerontology Nutrition Unit at the Royal Free Hospital Medical School, London has produced a wide range of research studies and accessible instructional materials on healthy diets in later life (Davies, 1988).

Contact address:

- Louise Davies, Gerontology Nutrition Unit, Royal Free Hospital School of Medicine, 21 Pond Street, London NW3 (tel: 01 794 4395)

The Sports Council began a campaign in 1983 to persuade people in the middle years of life to become involved in sport and physical recreation. Known as 50+ All to Play For, the main thrust is to build on existing local programmes and to encourage people to involve themselves in sport and active recreations. The Sports Council has prepared seven leaflets and audio-visual materials aimed at the public, and an Organisers' Manual of ideas and suggestions. This provides an impressive list of organisations that can assist and a useful list of information materials.

Contact address:

- The Sports Council, 16 Upper Woburn Place, London WC1H OQP (tel: 01 388 1277)

The Granton Community Health Project is an action research project into community approaches to health issues. It has included a Pensioners Swim Club, a range of summer activities, a health course for the elderly at a sheltered housing scheme, and the formation of an elderly persons' forum.

Contact address:
- Jane Jones, Granton Community Health Project, c/o Lothian Health Board, 11 Drumsheugh Gardens, Edinburgh EH3 7QQ

The Lothian Regional Council Community Education Service has been active in following the Scottish Sports Council's advocacy for active participation in some form of sport and physical recreation. It established a working group on Educational Opportunities for Older People which has set up a large number of pilot projects in central Scotland. It has also developed information packs, *Keep Warm This Winter*, to counter the problems of inadequately heated homes.

Contact address:
- Community Education Service, Lothian Regional Council, 40 Torphichen Street, Edinburgh EH3 8JJ (tel: 031 222 9292)

The Women's Royal Voluntary Service has taken several initiatives concerned to improve nutrition among elderly people, such as a project supported by the London Borough of Enfield to make available for purchase in luncheon clubs complete frozen meals, or the availability of store cupboard foods in WRVS-run clubs. The WRVS also arranges local authority or voluntary transport to enable immobile elderly people to visit shops and choose their own foods.

Contact address:
- WRVS, 17 Old Park Lane, London W1 (tel: 01 499 6040)

Support to Carers

The Alzheimer's Disease Society, the British Association for Service to the Elderly and the National Council for Carers and Their Elderly Dependants have all taken great interest in the development of respite care, support groups and other means for assisting carers and thereby enabling frail elderly people to continue to be supported in their own or their relatives' homes. The Informal Caring Support Unit based at the King's Fund Centre and supported since 1985 by the HEA and DoH has produced an excellent range of information and training materials including guides for carers, training programmes for professionals and guidelines for policy-makers and service providers.

Contact addresses:
- Alzheimer's Disease Society, Bank Buildings, Fulham Broadway, London SW6 1EP (tel: 01 381 3177)

- British Association for Service to the Elderly, 3 Keele Farmhouse, Keele, Staffordshire ST5 5AR (tel: 0782 627800)

- National Council for Carers, 29 Chilworth Mews, London W2 3RG (tel 01 724 7776)

- Informal Caring Support Unit, King's Fund Centre, 126 Albert Street, London NW1 7NF (tel 01 267 6111)

The Team for the Elderly at St Mary Abbott's Hospital, Chelsea (see above) has developed in conjunction with the Alzheimer's Disease Society both a support group for carers of elderly confused people, a Course for Carers, and a Carers' Information Day. Fife Health Board has produced a well-received comprehensive guide for carers of dementia suffers. It has been reproduced by Age Concern Scotland in conjunction with the Board and the Alzheimer's Disease Society under the title *Coping with Dementia: A Handbook for Carers*.

Contact address:
- Age Concern Scotland, 33 Castle Street, Edinburgh EH2 3DN (tel: 031 225 5000)

Attitudes and Self-Esteem

Many of our discussions touched on the importance of the attitudes of elderly people towards their own health and towards professionals and organisations in the health field. Various references were made, for example, to the passivity, resignation and deference found among some elderly people. The understanding that health is improvable at any age was said to be uncommon among elderly people. Some initiatives to combat inappropriate attitudes and to encourage a more positive approach to one's own health have been taken by health, social service and educational professionals. In Scotland particularly there has been a great deal of interest in establishing elderly people's forums. The Scottish Health Education Group (SHEG) has reported the existence of over 30 such forums in Strathclyde under the umbrella of the Strathclyde Elderly Forum. They promote the health of those involved and have run welfare rights campaigns. In Ayr over 30 self-help groups focusing on opportunities in retirement have grown up with the assistance of 'seed-corn' funding and organisational help from the SHEG, the Manpower Services Commission community programme, Age Concern Scotland and the New Horizons Trust. Many of the groups are specifically concerned with promoting physical health and morale.

Contact address:
- Opportunities in Retirement, Room 33, Ayr Academy, Fort Street, Ayr (tel: 0292 260086)

Self-actualisation is a strong motivation of the rapidly growing University of the Third Age Movement in Britain. While health promotion is only a minor element of its activities, popular and successful courses associated with fitness and health have been organised.

Contact address:
- U3A, 6 Parkside Gardens, London SW19 5EY

The Centre for Policy on Ageing takes a broad and practical interest in the promotion of positive attitudes in retirement. Its recent publications explore pilot initiatives in various parts of the country, including the work of the Niccol Centre in Cirencester (Armstrong, Midwinter and Wynne-Harley, 1987; Midwinter, 1982).

Contact addresses:
- Centre for Policy on Ageing, 25-31 Ironmonger Row, London EC1V 3QP (tel: 01 253 1787)

- Niccol Centre, Brewery Court, Cirencester, Gloucestershire (tel: 0285 67181)

LOCAL ORGANISATIONS

Local Government: Social Services Departments
Elderly at Risk Projects
Some Social Services Departments have tried various approaches to identifying vulnerable elderly people living in the community. Kent has established an Elderly at Risk Project which is conducting research into these issues in association with the District Health Authority.
Contact address:
- Jill Reece, Elderly at Risk Project, 49/50 Marsham Street, Maidstone, Kent ME14 1HH (tel: 0622 55706)

Innovations in Day Centres
The Beverley Rural Team of Humberside Social Services in 1985 introduced a mobile day centre, comprising a towing minibus and a trailer day centre. It visits five locations one day each week, serving up to 12 elderly people living in each catchment spread among the remoter villages of the Yorkshire Wolds. Unlike the existing village clubs and social centres which service relatively fit and mobile elderly people, this facility is designed for people with a need for high levels of domiciliary support. It offers rehabilitation work. Attenders include stroke victims, those confined to wheelchairs and

people suffering from diabetes, blindness, deafness and Parkinson's disease: the average age is in the mid-80s. The organisers report positive attitudes towards the facility by its clients, stress that the scheme should not be seen as better but rather as complementary to static rural day centres, and state that the additional expenditure on maintaining the service caters well for people of often a high level of infirmity (Reed, 1987).

Derbyshire Social Services Department is piloting day resource centres which seek to provide an integrated network of day services, domiciliary services, field work and medical services. One group has been established in association with the Housing Department and meets twice weekly in a local authority sheltered housing scheme (Thompson, 1987). It seeks to complement domiciliary and fieldwork services by providing: care to disabled elderly people whose carers require periods of respite; day care to socially isolated housebound elderly people; a personalised care service for disabled elderly people unable to benefit from domiciliary support; and a rehabilitation service for those requiring specialist or multidisciplinary services.

Health Authorities (including Primary Health Care)
Screening

This topic has been extensively debated by several medical colleges and groups and there is an extensive and authoritative literature (Department of Health and Social Security, 1987; Freer, 1985; Royal College of General Practitioners, 1981; Taylor and others, 1983). The Team for Elderly People at St Mary Abbott's Hospital, London, has developed case finding and a home visiting service for elderly people at risk (see above). A screening programme of elderly people has been initiated by health visitors and commenced in several districts of Lothian Health Board.

Day Hospitals

Day hospitals have been established for many years, but variations of the model are evident in recent innovations. The Department of Services for the Elderly at St James's Hospital, Milton, Portsmouth has organised a peripatetic team of nurses, an occupational therapist, two hospital consultants, a clerical assistant and volunteer workers. It visits four different centres, based on old people's homes, each week. Its advantages include the reduction of travelling time and inconvenience, the circumvention of the unwillingness to attend geriatric hospitals, and flexibility in organising a diversity of health, social and volunteer services.

Another recent development is the day hospital at Dilke Hospital in the Forest of Dean. It provides rehabilitation and assessment facilities during the week for 17 patients, but until recently was unused at weekends. Gloucester Health Authority has cooperated with local volunteers in opening the premises as a social centre at weekends. Voluntary transport, nursing and general practitioner on-call services have been organised and the additional costs met by the health authority (Dobbs and Clayton, 1987).

Health Promotion

East Dorset Health Authority took an initiative in health promotion for the elderly by creating a part-time post of Health Promotion Facilitator for the Bournemouth area in July 1986 (Jones, 1987). Several lines of action were developed, including courses and seminars for health authority and residential and nursing home professionals, the organisation of workshops for carers, assistance in the organisation of health fairs, and the mounting of display materials and the staffing of an information desk to form a Health in Retirement Centre for a six month period (from 19 October 1987) in Poole Central Library.

Training: The Use of Drugs

Age Concern Scotland have commissioned a 20 minute tape/slide programme on Older People and Their Medicines. Produced at the Department of Medical Illustration, University of Aberdeen, it concentrates on why the elderly person is particularly at risk from the mismanagement of drugs. It is intended for community health service workers, general practitioners, health visitors, junior hospital staff, medical students, nurses, occupational therapists, social workers and the general public. (Serial 84-431, £50 +VAT).

Contact address:
- Graves Medical Audiovisual Library, Holly House, 220 New London Road, Chelmsford, Essex CM2 9BJ (tel: 0245 83351).

Housing Authorities, Associations and Agencies

The Anchor Housing Trust has a Training Division which organises day meetings and courses for housing agency project workers and staff who are dealing with the housing concerns of elderly people. Recent topics include 'Planning and launching an agency service', 'Working with elderly owner occupiers', and 'Monitoring and evaluation of local projects'. Among the Trust's many housing-related activities, recent projects in association with district health authorities (for example, Lancaster, Staffordshire, South Manchester, Nottingham and Tower Hamlets) specifically to accommodate frail elderly people previously resident in long-stay mental hospitals have direct health dimensions. These schemes parallel this and other housing

associations' extra-care sheltered housing schemes for frail people.
Contact address:
- Anchor Housing Trust, Oxenford House, 13/15 Magdalen Street, Oxford OX1 3BP (tel: 0865 722261)

Home Heating Costs and Insulation

The excess of winter mortality in Britain and its association with low room temperatures has been mentioned at several points in this report. Action to counteract this problem is required at all levels, from targeting and financing of home improvement grants by central governments, to the local provision of advice and practical assistance to individual elderly people. At the local level initiatives have been taken in this field by local authority housing departments, community health councils, and voluntary bodies.

In Newcastle-Upon-Tyne the voluntary body Neighbourhood Energy Action has been assisting elderly people insulate their own homes.
Contact address:
- Neighbourhood Energy Action, 2/4 Bigg Market, Newcastle-Upon-Tyne NE1 1UW

Educational Authorities and Institutions

Many new developments in gerontological education and professional training are occurring during the later 1980s. Their impact on the health of elderly people will necessarily be in the long term but the training courses for nurses, residential and nursing care staff and sheltered housing wardens may have fairly direct impacts. The Centre for Environmental and Social Studies of Ageing (CESSA) at the Polytechnic of North London has been commissioned by the Department of Health to develop courses for care staff. The Institute of Housing has been primarily responsible for the development of a national wardens' certificated course which is now being taught at several further education centres in Britain.
Contact addresses:
- CESSA, Polytechnic of North London, Ladbroke House, Highbury Grove, London N5 2AD (tel: 01 607 2789 ext 5082)

- Institute of Housing, 9 White Lion Street, London N1 9XJ (tel: 01 278 2705)

The Scottish Health Education Group has organised short courses for professionals on Enabling Independence in Old Age (1985) and is planning another on Dementia (1988) to be followed up at the local level by multidisciplinary in-service courses. Age Concern Scotland has produced a *Training Resources Pack for Groups Helping Older People* (1986). The Royal Institute of Public Health and Hygiene (RIPHH) has been running seminars for those involved in menu planning and catering for elderly people in residential care.

Contact address:
- RIPHH, 28 Portland Place, London W1 (tel: 01 580 2731)

NATIONAL ORGANISATIONS AND INSTITUTIONS

National bodies, from departments of state to consumer associations, operate on many levels and their efforts towards facilitating self-care, improving professional practice and developing local services have already been mentioned. At the national level, however, several activities play an important part in health promotion. Advocacy, policy debate and development, education and communication, and the promotion and reform of training are all important functions of national bodies.

The British government has recently sponsored several reviews and reports on the health and social services. They put management and financial issues to the forefront. The present government is antipathetic towards egalitarian and universal free access models of health and social service provision but the long-term goals of a wide range of its policies, from the stimulation of community care services for elderly people requiring support in their own homes to reforms in primary health care, are to raise the overall physical and mental wellbeing and health of the population. The recent Cumberledge, Primary Health Care White Paper, Griffiths and Wagner reports contain many recommendations and proposals with implications for the health of elderly people (Department of Health and Social Security, 1986; Secretaries of State for Social Services, Wales, Northern Ireland and Scotland, 1987; Griffiths, 1988; Wagner, 1988).

Britain has flourishing advocacy, policy development, fund-raising and training 'ginger groups', with Age Concern and Help the Aged being not only active and well-known in every district of the country but also vigorous in national councils and campaigns. Several of their publications with health dimensions have been cited. They are persistent in arguing for more attention to the needs and preferences of elderly people. One of the workshop group's recommended actions was that there should be a minister for the elderly. Interestingly, the recent Griffiths report recommends a re-organisation of social and health service responsibilities under a single national department in the form of a minister for community care.

Debates concerning the reform of residential, nursing home, domiciliary personal social services, and chronic health care facilities for elderly people in Britain are coming to a head. In the reform and evolution of policy, there are many well-informed and articulate representative and advocacy bodies. The rapidly growing interest in issues about elderly people by the broadcasting and publishing organisations will widen the contributions, but it remains true that the voice of elderly people themselves will be poorly represented. It is often remarked that in Britain elderly people have little coherence or influence as an interest group. If this is to change, national educational institutions also have a part to play in the introduction of materials on individual ageing, not least with respect to its health dimensions.

REFERENCES AND USEFUL READING

General and National Policy Documents

K Andrews and J C Brocklehurst (1987) *British Geriatric Medicine in the 1980s*. London, King Edward's Hospital Fund for London.

British Medical Association (1986) *All Our Tomorrows: Growing Old in Britain*. Board of Science and Education Report. London, BMA.

Department of Health and Social Security (1986) *Neighbourhood Nursing — A Focus for Care*. London, HMSO.

Kathryn Dean (1987) *Self Care and Health in Old Age*. London, Croom Helm.

R Griffiths (1985) *Community Care: Agenda for Action*, London, HMSO.

Health Education Council (1984) *A Programme of Education for Health in Old Age: A Consultation Document*. London, HEC.

B Isaacs (1985) *Recent Advances in Geriatric Medicine*. Edinburgh, Churchill Livingstone.

J Kinnaird, J Brotherston and J Williamson (eds) (1981) *The Provision of Care for the Elderly*. Edinburgh, Churchill Livingstone.

R Means and R Smith (1985) *The Development of Welfare Services for Elderly People*. London, Croom Helm.

J A Muir Gray (1982) *Better Health in Retirement*. Mitcham, Surrey, Age Concern England.

J A Muir Gray (undated) *A Policy for Health Promotion in Old Age*. Oxford, District Department of Community Health, The Radcliffe Infirmary.

Secretaries of State for Social Services, Wales, Northern Ireland and Scotland (1988). *Promoting Better Health*. London, HMSO.

I Sinclair (ed) (1988) *Residential Care: The Research Reviewed*. Literature Surveys commissioned by the Independent Review of Residential Care (Wagner committee). London, HMSO.

G Wagner (1988) *Residential Care: A Positive Choice* (The Wagner report). London, HMSO.

Self-Care: General

C Cloke (1984) *Community Health Initiatives for Older People: A Directory*. Mitcham, Surrey, Age Concern.

C Cloke and A R Payne (1985) 'Pensioners' Health Days'. In: F Glendenning (ed) *New Initiatives in Self-Health Care for the Elderly*. Stoke-on-Trent, Beth Johnson Foundation, pp 83-86.

Help the Aged (1988) *Take Care of Yourself: A Health Handbook for Older People*. London, Help the Aged and Winslow Press.

London Borough of Hammersmith and Fulham (1987) *The 1986 Health and Fun Festival: A Report by the Steering Group*. London, LBHF.

Susan Tester and Barbara Meredith (1987) *Ill informed? Information and Support for Elderly People in the Inner City*. London, Policy Studies Institute.

Self-Care: Nutrition, Alcohol and Smoking

British Nutrition Foundation (1986) *Nutrition and the Elderly*, Briefing Paper 9. London, British Nutrition Foundation.

Age Concern Scotland and Scottish Council on Alcohol (1987) *Alcohol and Older People: A Leaflet Prepared for Those Caring for Older People*. ACS and SCA.

Louise Davies (1988) *Easy Cooking for One or Two*. London, Penguin.

Scottish Health Education Coordinating Committee (1983) *Health Education in the Prevention of Smoking-Related Disorders*. SHECC.

Self-Care: Exercise and Fitness

P H Fentem and E J Bassey (1983) *50+: A Safe Approach for Leaders*. London, Sports Council (revised 1985).

R Gibbs (1981) *Exercise for the Over 50s*. London, J Norman.

Local Organisations: Social Services Departments

P Reed (1987) 'A Moving Day Centre Filled With Laughter'. *Social Work Today*, 26 January, pp 14-15 (Humberside Mobile Day Centre).

K Thompson (1987) 'A Climate of Care'. *Social Services Insight*, 17 July, pp 15-17 (Derbyshire resource centre).

Local Organisations: Health Authorities

A Dobbs and A Clayton (1987) 'Empty Saturdays Come to Life'. *Health Service Journal*, 22 January p 102 (Dilke Day Hospital).

L J Donaldson and A Odell (1986) *Aspects of the Health and Social Service Needs of Elderly Asians in Leicester: a Community Survey.* Leicester, Department of Community Health, University of Leicester.

Charles B Freer (1985) 'Geriatric Screening: A Reappraisal of the Preventive Strategies in the Care of the Elderly'. *Journal of the Royal College of General Practitioners*, 35 pp 288-290.

David C. Kennie (1986) 'Health Maintenance of the Elderly'. *Clinics in Geriatric Medicine* 2,1 pp 53-83.

S Kirkman (1987) 'Moving With the Times'. *New Society*, 13 March, p 27. (Portsmouth travelling day hospital).

Rex Taylor, G Ford and J H Barber (1983) 'The Elderly at Risk: A Critical Review of Problems and Progress in Screening and Case-Finding'. *Research Perspectives* No 6. Mitcham, Surrey, Age Concern England.

Royal College of General Practitioners (1981) *Health and Prevention in Primary Care*, Report 18. London, RCGP.

Norman Vetter, D A Jones and C R Victor (1984) 'Effect of Health Visitors Working with Elderly Patients in General Practice'. *British Medical Journal*, 288, pp 369-372.

Educational Authorities and Organisations

June Armstrong, E Midwinter and D Wynne-Harley (1987) *Retired Leisure: Four Ventures in Post-Work Activity*, Report 9. Centre for Policy on Ageing.

Hilary Kirkland (1987) *Educational Opportunities for Older People: A Training Resource Pack*. Edinburgh, Lothian Regional Council Community Education Service.

H Kirkland, C Pilley and J Rees (eds) (1985) *Older People: Developing Opportunities*. Edinburgh, Scottish Community Education Group.

Scottish Community Education Council (1987) *The Age of Opportunity: A Policy Statement on Community Education and Work with Older People in Scotland*. Edinburgh, SCEC.

University of the Third Age. *U3A DIY:* A resource pack to guide groups and individuals wishing to start a U3A or similar self-help educational project. U3A, 6 Parkside Gardens, London SW19. £5.00 including post and packing.

E Midwinter (1982) *Age is Opportunity: Education and Older People*, Policy Studies in Ageing, No 2. London, Centre for Policy on Ageing.

E Midwinter (1986) *Mutual Aid Universities*. London, Croom Helm.

CONCLUSION

Myths about ageing remain prevalent in society, in particular those which serve to medicalise ageing and subscribe to the 'burden of ageing' thesis. At the same time, there is a challenge — promoting health among older people — which by and large remains to be met. We have highlighted those organisations and interests which are well placed to meet the challenge, and have given illustrative practical examples of where, and of ways in which, health promotion is being pursued with enthusiasm and, where it has been established, some success.

The lack of evaluation and/or hard data in the field of health promotion in old age invites vigorous action. Sufficient knowledge has been accumulated to generate action by many sectors. There is some way still to go both in communicating what is desirable and possible, and in encouraging the implementation of initiatives designed to promote health. Our aim in this brief policy statement has been modest, namely, to offer pointers derived from practice and research. It is up to all of us to act upon these to secure the kind of future and life-style we want.

APPENDIX 1

Participants who attended the workshop held in Harrogate and the study group meeting held in London, to produce the consultation document:

Name and Organisation

Ms Rebecca Boyton,★☆
Health Worker,
Hostel for Homeless Single Men,
Arlington House, Camden Town, London

Dr Alan Butler,★☆
Senior Lecturer in Mental Health,
Department of Psychiatry,
University of Leeds

Ms Anne Clarke,★
Regional Development Officer,
National Council for Carers and their Elderly
    Dependants

Mr Christopher Cloke,★
Information Policy Officer,
Age Concern England

Mr Allin Coleman,★
Coordinator,
Centre for Health and Retirement Education

Dr June Crown,★☆
District Medical Officer,
Bloomsbury Health Authority

Dr Charles B Freer,★☆
Senior Lecturer in Primary Medical Care,
University of Southampton

Ms Emily Grundy,★☆
Lecturer in Social Gerontology,
King's College London (KQC)

Mr John Huntington,★☆
Assistant Director,
Continuing Education,
Health Education Authority

Ms Vera Ivers,★☆
Development Officer,
The Beth Johnson Foundation

Dr Bobbie Jacobson,*★☆
Registrar in Community Medicine,
St Leonard's London

Professor Margot Jefferys,★☆
Emeritus Professor of Medical Sociology,
University of London

Dr David Kennie,★
Consultant Physician in Geriatric Medicine,
The Royal Infirmary, Stirling

Dr Alastair MacDonald,★☆
Senior Lecturer in Psychogeriatrics,
United Medical and Dental Schools
(Guy's Campus)
Guy's Hospital, London

Dr John Mitchell,★☆
(Consultant) Unit General Manager,
Community Services Unit,
Waltham Forest Health Authority

Ms Caroline Oliver,★
Head of Public Relations,
Age Concern England

Miss Jill Reece,★☆
Project Officer for the Elderly,
Kent County Council

Dr Maureen Roberts,★☆
Edinburgh Breast Screening Clinic

Ms Phil Runciman,★☆
Lecturer in Nursing Studies,
Queen Margaret College, Edinburgh

Miss Jill Spratley,★☆
Lecturer in Continuing Education in
    Community Medicine,
London School of Hygiene and Tropical
    Medicine

Dr Rex Taylor,★☆
MRC Research Sociologist,
Glasgow

Dr Norman J Vetter,★☆
Director,
Research Team for the Care of the Elderly,
University of Wales

Worshop Organisers

Dr David J Hunter,
Health Policy Analyst,
King's Fund Institute

Dr Alex Kalache,
Senior Research Fellow,
Unit for Epidemiology of Ageing,
London School of Hygiene and Tropical
Medicine

Dr Tony Warnes,
Senior Research Associate,
Age Concern Institute of Gerontology,
King's College London

Secretaries

Sue Hicken,
Administrative/Information Assistant

Lorraine Cummings,
Secretarial Assistant,
Unit of Epidemiology of Ageing,
London School of Hygiene and Tropical
Medicine

Su Bellingham,
Secretary,
King's Fund Institute

Rachel Stuchbury,
Secretary,
Age Concern Institute of Gerontology,
King's College London

KEY

* Workshop Rapporteur
★ Harrogate (February 1987)
☆ London (April 1987)

Workshop on Health Promotion and Ageing, 4-6 February 1987, NHS Training and Studies Centre, Harrogate

PROGRAMME

Wednesday 4 February
10.30
Registration and coffee

11.00-12.30
Introductory session
(1) Health promotion — the concepts
   JILL SPRATLEY

(2) An international perspective
   JILL SPRATLEY

(3) Health Promotion and ageing
   ALEX KALACHE

(4) WHO Advisory Group Meeting
   "Effectiveness of Health Promotion for the
   Elderly", Canada, April 1986 —
   preliminary report
   ALEX KALACHE

(5) Setting the scene in Britain (I)
   JOHN HUNTINGTON

Discussion

12.30
Lunch

14.00-15.30
Setting the scene in Britain (II) — short
presentations based on the papers circulated
prior to the meeting. Each presentation will
be followed by discussion
REX TAYLOR
CHARLES FREER
NORMAN VETTER

15.30
Tea

16.00-17.30
Methodological issues — short presentations
based on papers circulated prior to the
meeting. Each presentation will be followed
by discussion
DAVID KENNIE
ALEX KALACHE (introducing Robert Kane's
paper)

55

18.15
Dinner

19.30-21.00
Setting the objectives
Structure for the rest of the workshop

Thursday 5 February
8.00-8.45
Breakfast

9.00
Small group work

10.30
Coffee

10.45
Plenary session: resetting the objectives

13.00
Lunch

14.00
Small group work

16.00
Plenary session

18.15
Dinner

19.30

Resetting the objectives: meeting of the main rapporteur and small group rapporteurs with the workshop organisers

Friday 6 February
8.00-8.45
Breakfast

9.00-10.30
Short presentations from group rapporteurs on outcomes from the small group work

Summary of group work outcomes
BOBBIE JACOBSON

10.30
Coffee

10.45
Small group work

12.00
Final plenary session to discuss the workshop and the second stage

13.00
Lunch

14.00
Workshop organisers to meet with main rapporteur and the rapporteurs from the small groups

APPENDIX 2

Participants of the national workshop held at the King's Fund Centre, London, on 5 October 1987.

NAME AND ORGANISATION

Miss J M Bennett
National Council for Carers and their Elderly Dependants

Mrs L Boardman
London Pensioner

Ms R Boyton
Health Worker,
United Kingdom Housing Trust Ltd

Professor J C Brocklehurst
Consultant Physician in Geriatric Medicine,
University of Manchester

Mrs J Burman
London Regional Officer, Association of Carers

Dr A Butler
Senior Lecturer in Mental Health, Department of Psychiatry,
University of Leeds

Ms A Clarke
Regional Development Officer,
National Council for Carers and their Elderly Dependants

Mr A Coleman
Coordinator,
Centre for Health and Retirement Education,
University of London

Dr H Curtis
Research and Project Officer,
British Medical Association

Miss L Dyer
Editor,
Physiotherapy Practice Journal

Dr C B Freer
Senior Lecturer in Primary Medical Care,
University of Southampton

Dr R Gibbins
Department of Social Services,
Royal County of Berkshire

Dr M Gill
Consultant Community Physician,
Grimsby District Health Authority

Ms L Gregory
Team for the Elderly,
St Mary Abbotts Hospital, London

Mrs E Grove
Occupational Therapy Officer,
Department of Health and Social Security

Ms E Grundy
Lecturer in Social Gerontology,
Age Concern Institute of Gerontology,
King's College London

Dr K Herbst
Policy Development Officer,
Mental Health Foundation

Mr R Hollingbery
Helen Hamlyn Foundation

Dr B Jacobson
Registrar in Community Medicine,
St Leonard's, London

Professor M Jeffreys
Emeritus Professor of Medical Sociology,
University of London

Ms C Jones
Health Visitors Association

Dr D C Kennie
Consultant Physician in Geriatric Medicine,
Forth Valley Health Board

Ms S Kontos
Acting District Chiropodist,
Bloomsbury Health Authority

Ms M Lewis
Pensioners' Link — Hackney

Dr B Lodge
Consultant Physician in Psychogeriatric Medicine,
Leicestershire Health Authority

Dr A MacDonald
Senior Lecturer in Psychogeriatrics,
United Medical and Dental Schools,
(Guy's Campus), Guy's Hospital

THE OTTAWA CHARTER

The first International Conference on Health Promotion, meeting in Ottawa this 21 day of November 1986, hereby presents this CHARTER for action to achieve Health for All by the year 2000 and beyond.

This conference was primarily a response to growing expectations for a new public health movement around the world. Discussions focused on the needs in industrialised countries, but took into account similar concerns in all other regions. It built on the progress made through the Declaration on Primary Health Care at Alma Ata, the World Health Organization's *Targets for Health for All* document, and the recent debate at the World Health Assembly on intersectoral action for health.

Health Promotion

Health promotion is the process of enabling people to increase control over, and to improve, their health. To reach a state of complete physical, mental and social wellbeing, an individual or group must be able to identify and to realise aspirations, to satisfy needs, and to change or cope with the environment. Health is, therefore, seen as a resource for everyday life, not the objective of living. Health is a positive concept emphasising social and personal resources, as well as physical capacities. Therefore, health promotion is not just the responsibility of the health sector, but goes beyond healthy lifestyles to wellbeing.

Prerequisites for Health

The fundamental conditions and resources for health are peace, shelter, education, food, income, a stable eco-system, sustainable resources, social justice and equity. Improvement in health requires a secure foundation in these basic prerequisites.

Advocate

Good health is a major resource for social, economic and personal development and an important dimension of quality of life. Political, economic, social, cultural, environmental, behavioural and biological factors can all favour health or be harmful to it. Health promotion action aims at making these conditions favourable through *advocacy* for health.

Enable

Health promotion focuses on achieving equity in health. Health promotion action aims at reducing differences in current health status and ensuring equal opportunities to *enable* all people to achieve their fullest health potential. This includes a secure foundation in a supportive environment, access to information, life skills and opportunities for making healthy choices. People cannot achieve their fullest health potential unless they are able to take control of those things which determine their health. This must apply equally to women and men.

Mediate

The prerequisites and prospects for health cannot be ensured by the health sector alone. More importantly, health promotion demands coordinated action by all concerned: by governments, by health and other social and economic sectors, by non-government and voluntary organisations, by local authorities, by industry and by the media. People in all walks of life are involved as individuals, families and communities. Professional and social groups and health personnel have a major responsibility to *mediate* between differing interests in society for the pursuit of health.

Health promotion strategies and programmes should be adapted to the local needs and possibilities of individual countries and regions to take into account differing social, cultural and economic systems.

Health Promotion Action Means:

Build Healthy Public Policy

Health promotion goes beyond health care. It puts health on the agenda of policy makers in all sectors and at all levels, directing them to be aware of the health consequences of their decisions and to accept their responsibilities for health.

Health promotion policy combines diverse but complementary approaches including legislation, fiscal measures, taxation and organisational change. It is coordinated action that leads to health, income and social policies that foster greater equity. Joint action contributes to ensuring safer and healthier goods and services, healthier public services, and cleaner, more enjoyable environments.

Health promotion policy requires the identification of obstacles to the adoption of healthy public policies in non-health sectors, and ways of removing them. The aim must be to make the healthier choice the easier choice for policy makers as well.

Create Supportive Environments

Our societies are complex and interrelated. Health cannot be separated from other goals. The inextricable links between people and their environment constitutes the basis for a socio-ecological approach to health. The overall guiding principle for the world, nations, regions and communities alike, is the need to encourage reciprocal maintenance — to take care of each other, our communities and our natural environment. The conservation of natural resources throughout the world should be emphasised as a global responsibility.

Changing patterns of life, work and leisure have a significant impact on health. Work and leisure should be a source of health for people. The way society organises work should help create a healthy society. Health promotion generates living and working conditions that are safe, stimulating, satisfying and enjoyable.

Systematic assessment of the health impact of a rapidly changing environment — particularly in areas of technology, work, energy production and urbanisation — is essential and must be followed by action to ensure positive benefit to the health of the public. The protection of the natural and built environments and the conservation of natural resources must be addressed in any health promotion strategy.

Strengthen Community Action

Health promotion works through concrete and effective community action in setting priorities, making decisions, planning strategies and implementing them to achieve better health. At the heart of this process is the empowerment of communities, their ownership and control of their own endeavours and destinies.

Community development draws on existing human and material resources in the community to enhance self-help and social support, and to develop flexible systems for strengthening public participation and direction of health matters. This requires full and continuous access to information, learning opportunities for health, as well as funding support.

Develop Personal Skills

Health promotion supports personal and social development through providing information, education for health and enhancing life skills. By so doing, it increases the options available to people to exercise more control over their own health and over their environments, and to make choices conducive to health.

Enabling people to learn throughout life, to prepare themselves for all of its stages and to cope with chronic illness and injuries is essential. This has to be facilitated in school, home, work and community settings. Action is required through educational, professional, commercial and voluntary bodies, and within the institutions themselves.

Reorient Health Services

The responsibility for health promotion in health services is shared among individuals, community groups, health professionals, health service institutions and governments. They must work together towards a health care system which contributes to the pursuit of health.

The role of the health sector must move increasingly in a health promotion direction, beyond its responsibility for providing clinical and curative services. Health services need to embrace an expanded mandate which is sensitive and respects cultural needs. This mandate should support the needs of individuals and communities for a healthier life, and open channels between the health sector and broader social, political, economic and physical environmental components.

Reorienting health services also requires stronger attention to health research as well as changes in professional education and training. This must lead to a change of attitude and organisation of health services, which refocuses on the total needs of the individual as a whole person.

Moving into the Future

Health is created and lived by people within the settings of their everyday life; where they learn, work, play and love. Health is created by caring for oneself and others, by being able to take decisions and have control over one's life circumstances, and by ensuring that the society one lives in creates conditions that allow the attainment of health by all its members.

Caring, holism and ecology are essential issues in developing strategies for health promotion. Therefore, those involved should take as a guiding principle that, in each phase of planning, implementation and evaluation of health promotion activities, women and men should become equal partners.

Commitment to Health Promotion

The participants in this conference pledge:

● to move into the arena of healthy public policy, and to advocate a clear political commitment to health and equity in all sectors;

● to counteract the pressures towards harmful products, resource depletion, unhealthy living conditions and environments, and bad nutrition; and to focus attention on public health issues such as pollution, occupational hazards, housing and settlements;

- to respond to the health gap within and between societies, and to tackle the inequities in health produced by the rules and practices of these societies;

- to acknowledge people as the main health resource, to support and enable them to keep themselves, their families and friends healthy through financial and other means, and to accept the community as the essential voice in matters of its health, living conditions and wellbeing;

- to reorient health services and their resources towards the promotion of health; and to share power with other sectors, other disciplines and most importantly with people themselves;

- to recognise health and its maintenance as a major social investment and challenge and to address the overall ecological issue of our ways of living.

The conference urges all concerned to join them in their commitment to a strong public health alliance.

Call For International Action

The Conference calls on the World Health Organization and other international agencies to advocate the promotion of health in all appropriate forums and to support countries in setting up strategies and programmes for health promotion.

The Conference is firmly convinced that if people in all walks of life, non-governmental and voluntary organisations, governments, the World Health Organization and all other bodies concerned join forces in introducing strategies for health promotion, in line with the moral and social values that form the basis of this CHARTER, Health For All by the year 2000 will become a reality.